COUNTRY KITTENS

AF430490

On a warm spring day, MiMi was gardening in the yard. She heard Meowing and crying from the barn. As she got closer, she saw two baby kittens feeding from their mother's milk. MiMi was very excited and ran quickly back into the house to share the news with her granddaughter Nina Rose and her grand nieces, Valentina and Liliana.

Barn Kittens

New Kittens

Mimi informed the children that a new family of kittens were in the barn She began to sing," There are little kittens in the barn. If you wake them, if you shake them, they get very loud. They children were widely excited. Dancing and squealing with delight. Let's go outside Mimi.

Mimi also called grandma and Nanny to come and join the children to see the new litter of kittens. All family members were so delighted.

Baby Kittens

"The kittens are so beautiful." Everyone replied. They smell of soft baby breath and sweet morning dew, mixed with mother's milk and a little kitten poop. Three black kittens with blue eyes and three kittens with green eyes. Absolutely picture-purfect: Pink-rosey noses and cherry red lips. Bundles of soft cotton-ball fur, with chubby cherub bellies and perfectly-shaped padded hot-pink paws.

The only exception of the grey kittens are blessed with double, six-digit front paws.

Feral Cats

As the little kittens began to grow, it began harder and harder to separate the little kittens from them mom and dad. It was difficult to separate the kittens as they came from "outdoors" families of cats, called, " feral cats." Feral cats are "non-domestic cats. " Non-domestic cats are felines (cats) who live outside in the wild or, in this case, on a farm with other animals in a barn." It was also difficult for Mimi and Grandma to afford to feed all of the kittens.

Therefore, it was time to see if we could find families who would be interested in adopting some of the kittens.

Summer Kitties

    Mimi and Grandma advertised to friends and family on facebook about the kittens; in the hopes they may like to adopt some of the kittens.

    On a muggy July evening two of Mimi's friends and cousins, Julie and Jim, came to visit the kittens and try to catch them and get one of them home. Jim tried several times to get them in a comfy box they lined with a blanket, food, and soft toy. Jim chased the kittens through the farm. Under the bushes, the trees and the coral. But to no avail.

Ferocious Felicity

Catch The Kittens

Upon exiting the coral, Jim and Julie became scared when seeing the mother cat hissing at them--A midnight black cat with almond piercing eyes-,Mimi and Grandma exclaimed, "This is mommy cat, "Ferrocious Felicity!" Felicity roaring like a female tiger," Hissed and then raised her paws in a karate chop and said, "STAY AWAY FROM MY KITTIES OR I'LL SCRATCH YOUR EYES OUT." Jim and Julie slowly moved back from the cat and kittens and into their truck.

They suggested that MiMi and Grandma call the local animal rescues, and feral cat

Mommy The Lion Cat

Human animal shelters to help rescue, and give the family of cats proper veterinary care so that they can be adopted into families.

The next morning, Mimi called the local nimal shelter who came to provide food for Ferrocious Felicility and her kittens. They did not want to set up traps because they felt the family of kittens were safe where they were with Mimi and Grandma.

As the heat of August came, the kittens beame very frisky and more independent from their mother. They were eating and drining on their own,

Black and Grey Kittens

Stucky

One of the Kittens is Missing

Mimi went about her usual morning, She went outside to feed the six kittens and their ferocious mom. Mimi saw only two grey kittens and three black kittens. When she went into the the bulk-head of the three-hundred year old colonial dirt-cellar, she could here loud cries and meows coming from the top of the stairwell. Mimi tried with all her might to climb to the very top of the stairs where an opening was, but she was not able to break open the cement underneath the wooden bulk-head. She tried several tactics, such as putting food up in the opening of the bulk head but the kitten would not come out.

Crying Kittens

HELP IS ON THE WAY

Mimi called several family and friends over to help her get the little grey kitten out. Since he was truly stuck in the "bulkhead," we decided to give him the name, "Stucky."

Suzy, Peter, and Isaiah, who adopted the kittens, grandparent kitties, Scooter and Scoottie," came over to dismantle the upstairs flooring and check the attic, in the hopes they could free little "Stucky."

Peter placed a large hole in the top of the stairs, to make it easier for "Stucky" to get out of the bulkhead, but he just was too scared to jump down."

Family Unity

After four days of not being able to get "Stucky" out of the bulkhead, all of the kittens along with their mom and, finally, their dad, Big Bob cat, all were waiting together in the hallway, near the stairs where they could hear their baby sibling, crying for help.

The family was now bonding with their dad. They were very upset and unable to eat. The family of cats waited to nightfall until they finally left the stairs to the bulkhead.

Mimi decided, she had to act fast and call the animal control officer to come and help Stucky.

Grandparent Cats with Isaiah

Daddy Big Bob Cat

Sibling Female Kittens

While we waited for the animal control officer to come and assist in getting Stucky out.

All of the little granddaughters were also upset that Stucky was missing. Therefore, Mimi and and grandma decided to allow the children to name all the kittens.

Valentina, the eldest granddaughter decided to name the firstborn female black kitten, ZuZu. Now it was Nina's turn to name a kitten, she selected, Zimba, for the second-born male kitten. Now it was Liliana, the youngest grandchild to name a kitten. She selected, " Dutchess," for the third-born black female kitten.

Mommy and Family of Kittens

Sibling Male Kittens

The little girls took turns until all the kittens were named. Valentina named the fourth kitten, a cuddly black and furry male, "cuddles."

Nina, who just got a new puppy at home decided to name the next fluffy black male kitten, "Snuggles."

The last grey kitten was named "Stucky," by Grandma, since he got stuck in the bulkhead for exactly six days

Finally, Liliana named, the last grey kitten, a male, "Duke."

Stucky is Freed

After an entire week of trying to free Stucky, Mimi and Grandma began to lose hope of every seeing Stucky again. His family waited for six days. Finally, Liza, the cat officer, cme to assist Mimi. Stucky's cries were very faint but she could still hear him. Liza brought a kitten trap with anchovies which she placed underneath the bulkhead. Within an hour, Stucky was in the kitten trap.

Sadly, she never told Mimi, she would be trapping all the other kittens and their mom, Ferrocious Felicity, who was hiding beneath Great Grandfather's cadillac.

The Family of Cats is Missing

Mimi and Nanny (Great Grandma) were having a difficult time trying to care and feed the new family of 2 mommy and daddy cats and 6 kittens along with their two adult, domestic cats, Bella and Zoe.

But they were willing to care for the cats until they could be adopted by caring families.

Unfortunately, the cats would need to be spayed, neutered and receive vaccines.

- ***Spayed/Neutered:*** When a cat has surgery so that he/she cannot have anymore kittens.

Bella

Bella, 15-year old domestic long-haired cat

Zoe

Zoe, our 20 year-old Flexible Flier cat.

Ferrocious Felicity is Pregnant

Mimi and Grandma became very upset that the family of cats was now gone. They waited for two days to see why the cats hadn't returned.

So Mimi called the animal officer to find out what happened to the family of cats and kittens, She was told the kittens and cats were taken to the veterinarian, Dr. Felix, to be examined and receive their vaccines.

Mimi was then told that "***Ferrocious Felicity,*** is pregnant with another litter of kittens.

- ***Veterinarian:*** An animal doctor

Mimi Adopts a Cat

Mimi and Grandma explained to the children that the family of cats and kittens had been taken to the veterinarian.

The very next day, Grandma and Mimi visited the shelter and requested adoption of at least one kitten.

In the afternoon, Mimi received a large black kitten who quickly ran into the bathroom. Nanny was very annoyed because the kitten was so large. He blocked her entrance into the bathroom and she could not take a bat! "Oh dear, "What do we do cried Mimi and Nanny?"

Daddy Bob Cat Returns

"This cat is not a kitten." Mimi and Nanny said. "He's just too big." I can't get him out ouf the sink. And then Daddy cat jumped into the tub.

Finally, mommy came and took the cat back to the shelter. Mommy then requested that we all could adopt a kitten when the new litter is born.

"But we each want a kitten, cried the little girls. "Yes. You will all get a baby kitten as soon as Mommy cat, Felicity has her new litter." Said Mimi.

Welcome Fall

Halloween Cats

    Just before Halloween, The shelter called to inform Mimi and grandma the new litter of kittens had arrived Another litter of 5 black and white kittens and two calico kittens. The children were very excited to visit the shelter and pick out a kitten to adopt.

    When they arrived at the shelter directly across from the pumpkin patch, the family of cats and kittens were eagerly awaiting. They were purring and meowing. Happy to see their adoptive family again.

Happy Halloween

NEW BABY KITTENS

Calico kittens are kittens of many colors:

About the Author

Anita Mello Baddeley, B.A., MEd. Attended Freetown Schools and was a graduate of Bristol Community College where she worked as an EDP Operator for almost 16 years. She then received her B.A. in Psychology and MEd from Cambridge College. Ms. Mello Baddeley also attended Bridgewater State University where she received a Paralegal Certification and post-graduate studies in teacher certification.

Anita was a former Sped Educator, Enmployment Specialist for disabled students and adults. She then became a Children's book writer for Amazon back in 2015 with her four non-fiction books: ***A Pony For Christmas, Dogs and The Good They Do For Us, Belinda The Bunny, and Valentina and The Turtle Doves.***

Ms. Mello-Baddeley is the grandmother of Valentina and Liliana Landim and the Godmother of Evalina Rose (Nina) Baptista.

She is interested in pursuing her post-gradiuate/doctoral studies in Psychology,

www.ingramcontent.com/pod-product-compliance
Lightning Source LLC
Chambersburg PA
CBHW042058110726
48006CB00002B/448